A Broken Escalator Still Isn't the Stairs

A Broken Escalator Still Isn't the Stairs

CHUCK CARLISE

Concrete Wolf Poetry Chapbook Series

ISBN 978-0-9797137-5-0

Design by Tonya Namura

Cover art: "tower of babel 7" by Andrew Rottner
from the series *After Flood All Earth Talk As One...*
written and illustrated by Andrew Rottner
Copyright Super Classy Publishing 2007

Author photo by Chuck Carlise

Concrete Wolf Poetry Chapbook Series

Concrete Wolf
PO Box 1808
Kingston, WA 98346

http://ConcreteWolf.com

ConcreteWolf@yahoo.com

dicatively. The same; the same thing.
trengthened by *all*: see ALL C. 5.

WYCLIF *Serm*. Sel. Wks. I. 26 It is al oon to seie þat
lis ben þus sacrid. *c* 1420 *Pallad. on Husb*. IX. 204
t and May in houris lengthe are oon. *c* 1430 *Pilgr.*
ʒode I. xlix. (1869) 29 For j seyd not in alle places,
e times; and þat is not oon. 1584 R. SCOT *Discov*.
v. ix. (1886) 87 It [witchcraft] is all one with
1631 R. BOLTON *Comf. Affl. Consc*. vi. (1635) 36
e to Him to make an Angell, or an Ant. *c* 1670
ial. Comm. Laws 50 Which is also one as if he were
nself. 1816 J. WILSON *City of Plague* I. iii. 271 All
one to me. 186. DASENT *Story Burnt Njal* II. 402
tale and silver by weight was all one.

e in mind, feeling, intention, or bearing;
on, harmonious, at one.

R. BRUNNE *Chron*. (1810) 24 At haly kirke's fayth

A Broken Escalator Still Isn't the Stairs

*

To say one is missing is to talk of perspective. You say, she is not with me. You say, he is not where I want him. There are footprints on the trail, & they lead somewhere you are nervous to follow. Stare long enough & they code like glyphs, like a language you feel you ought to know. Do they track toward you or away? You say, I will wait here. You say, I will follow them out. Words bring you no closer to knowing. Who were you to own these eyes at all?

*

For the first few weeks, I can't sleep through the night. I awake to her voice like a farmer in a minefield 20 years after the war, who steps three inches to the left & in his heel feels earthshake for the tiniest instant, before what's past comes to take him.

*

On the flight, I nod off trying to remember the circumference of the halo my arms made circling her shoulders & chest. 'You kiss me like a baby sometimes,' she says, watching us in the mirror while I bury my face in the soft shiver behind her ear. Don't tell me I am making this up. She laughs & closes her eyes, & I'd sooner drop out of the sky in a cloud of ash. Why would you tell me that?

❋

This is a story about remembering: neurons pop like an invasion, like a firestorm, sparks & shrapnel lighting the dark space in every direction. You don't see them. You see because of them.

*

Ocean rolls & twists seven miles beneath us, so remote it's an act of faith just believing it's there.

*

To say one is *missing* is to cede responsibility, to create distance, passive observation. You wake in a room to men paving the street – smell of tarsmoke & blacktop. May as well be anywhere. Somewhere else, the streetlamps flicker on, the sun beginning to fade. Through the window now, a screech of gears – then shouting, a crowd. Gasoline in the air. Something frantic. In that dusk, no one's saying, *he's far away*. They're saying, *he left*.

*

A man on the train calls Rome an endless excavation. Down the coast a few hours south, I think the world itself is the opposite. All our dynamite & digging, sloughing away stones, while the Earth liquefies & spreads, cools to blowing dust. Where is Carthage now?

*

In this country, I'm told, when they dub an actor's voice, the double stays with him for life. Some grow famous, cast shadows with bodies no one ever sees. Others fade like a daydream interrupted by carhorn, tiresqueal – a thing that will always ride shotgun to an image that was never its own.

*

Heat lightning in the clouds, like camera flashes in all directions. The air silent & strange. Imagine: your whole identity built on erasing another's voice.

*

The square of dry asphalt beneath a parked car in the rain. More.

*

To say one is *missing* is to insist on the physics of the body. In occupied space. The stairstep's center dip. The duomo's steeple points. There is heat & there is color, but we measure them by degrees. The inflection of a voice in a crowded hall. How accusing is its tone? How playful? Demand an answer, a resolution. Demand to know. Believe someone was there to begin with.

*

Statues of the Virgin everywhere – her shrines
wreathed in votive candles & chipped paint. They
rise from retaining walls, flank balcony gates –
shallow platforms cut from the corners of buildings.
Our Lady of Perpetual Watching. Holy Mother of
Never Being Alone. She is ragged, crumbling smile
on what's left of her lips. I turn a corner. Another.
She never stops. Queen of Surveillance. Of Having
Nowhere to Hide.

*

Walls tell the same story in every room. Outside,
night is a cloth dropping over a lampshade – radiant
dimming, a nervous erasure. A thing happening far
away. This is where you are, the walls say. It's all
they ever say.

*

Nothing is ever forgotten, just misplaced. The rhythm of reciting your first address, scent of the yew trees in that yard. On the street below, a man with your father's hands steps off the curb, squints toward a cathedral up the hill. (Life as a drawer of postcards – each moment distinct, regular, scattered among all the others.) When he turns the corner the sky is a cloudless dome. You already have no words to describe it.

*

Two 12-year-old girls shoot through minefield
Milazzo traffic on a bleating white scooter; streetlights
catch the broken glass by an overflowing dumpster
the striking sanitation men haven't gathered in weeks.
In the piazza, an old man in three piece suit paces
back & forth alone.

*

To say one is *missing* is to speak without context, without here-&-now. A state of being with no edges or agency. The ceiling collapses in the storm – plaster & sheetrock, splintered wedges of polished wood. You learn to live against the wall, on the perimeter, with need. Not to long for, but simply to be without. In a state of absence. Of *missing*.

*

Open water is never actually open water. On a long enough horizon, there is always rock, dust, root to hem it in. Still, in the rutted blue between the last buoy & the distant ghost of land, it's easy to believe in flatness & empty air. When the volcano's shape darkens from haze to shadow to obsidian & pumice beach, I am more relieved than I'd expected. The absoluteness of its presence. The blackness & sulpher & spit. The utter lack of doubt.

*

Her voice is still a tiny flash of light – bright enough to pull my eyes from the road; never lasting long enough to leave any residue of warmth.

*

The rain tonight, a fever breaking.

*

To say one is *missing* is to acknowledge how the objects in the room have lost meaning – how they assemble themselves so precisely for a world that does not exist. How absurd the arrangement of pens on the desk, the reflection of light on the windowglass. When you enter a room, you already know the quiet. You know it & know it.

*

When Vesuvius opened its eyes, they say, ash teemed in the sky for hours. They watched from the foothills, stood in the wide streets, holding hands. Prayer is a kind of transference of agency & no one fled as the heavens grew dark & heavy. When the canopy collapsed, the cinder & dust didn't squall from the clouds as smoking rain, but burst across the valley, swallowed the city like a tidal wave.

✳

Smoke & mirrors, they call it when what's taken's not really gone. *Now you see it, now you don't.* So many ways to hope. Once upon a time, a city snuffed meant nothing left – the great Punic empire burned to cinders, fields salted to years of dust. When the Earth ends a story, it's more of a trade, a hiding game – rabbits, tophats. Catania's black sidewalks of magma & ash; paintings on the brothel walls unearthed in Pompeii.

*

Snap a picture of the grasses ahead – impossibly green where the trail crosses over. Vertigo of the moment – steep hillside scattered with rocks. Sometimes it's hard to believe you'll ever die.

*

To say one is missing is to build walls around air. To claim ownership, to isolate. Talk in states of being, not becoming. Remember it as a stack of bordered slides. You are shivering in the dark while she stands to leave & the streetlight briefly forms a halo behind her head. Your shoulders rattle & you rewrite the story as it happens. Not this slide, another. Not a halo, a hole.

*

An empty chair at the table? No. *A phonecall gone unanswered?* No. *A half-sleep reach across an empty bed?* No. None of these.

*

Claustrophobia is a train window fogsmeared with dust & spores like snowflake crystals. An island: an organism remaking itself. When we pass through the tunnel, the skin sheds to palm stalks & fruit-heavy prickly-pear, feudal olive plots abandoned & overfull, their branches in the air like mangled hands. Snakeskin & chrysalis are broken by bacteria, carried off by nesting sparrows. I sift rockdust through my fingers, spread a layer on the floor by my feet. I am alive & the island moves below.

*

To say one is missing is to suggest search, possibility, the transience of loss. To say one is missing is to create order & correctness. Then break it. To admit regret, desperation. To be humbled, even when no one else can know.

*

We've all suffered enough, haven't we? As with most things, it's more a question of 'when.' (Venice racing to become the sea again, a tower tipping fractions by the year.) Back in Portland, I'd jog around Tabor like a dog in the sun – eyes wide, licking the Douglas Fir scent from the air. When Hood blows its crown again, this is the fracture that will bury my house in flaming iron & lead. These days I want to disappear just to know that I can. That I can come back in the end.

*

The climb takes all morning – rim finally yielding by noon. White sulfer smoke in the air, singeing & acrid – a bouquet of lace breezing from dust-dry rock. The crater is shallower than it seems from below – a shot-glass of ash & cracked mudstone. The sky at eye-level. It's all around – an unbroken field of blue. Impossible to say where it ends & the sea begins.

Thanks / Acknowledgements / Notes

I owe much thanks to all of the mentors and colleagues who contributed thoughtful advice and encouragement as I assembled this chapbook, in particular: Sam Amadon, Mel Barrett, Sean Bishop, Liz Countryman, Mark Doty, Ryler Dustin, Laura-Eve Engle, Nick Flynn, Mat Johnson, Janine Joseph, Eric Higgins, Tony Hoagland, Sophie Klahr, Eric Kocher, D.A. Powell, Martha Serpas, Bruce Smith, and Mathew Zapruder. This book would also be inconceivable to me if I had not had the good fortune of learning from Bob Davis, j. Kastely, Sandra McPherson, Susannah Mintz, Gary Snyder, John Wagner, and Alan Williamson.

Also, I am indebted to James Bertelino, Lana Hechtman Ayers and Concrete Wolf Press for their faith and patience; Andy Rottner for his terrific cover image; and to the Tin House Summer Writer's Workshop, University of Houston, Labratorio Linguistico, Dorothy Sargent Rosenberg Foundation, and Writers in the Schools for helping send me back to Sicily and survive the writing/editing months that followed.

And finally, for the many other ways I've been supported along the way, I can only offer my endless thanks to my parents, Chuck and Cathy Carlise; and my gratitude to James Austin, Amanda Fields, Kristin Kearns, Mattie Bamman, Craig Arnold, Russel Swenson, Joe Carlise, Maggie Plummer, Calorgero Carlisi, Accursia Catanese, and D., all of whom either helped facilitate my finishing this project, or were on my mind while I did.

Vignettes from this sequence first appeared as a lyric essay in *Pleiades* under the same title. They are reprinted here with gratitude.

Pg. 20 borrows a phrase from Rauan Klassnick's *Holy Land*.

✳

Chuck Carlise was born in Canton, Ohio, on the first Flag Day of the Jimmy Carter Era, and has lived in a dozen states and two continents in the last decade. He is the author of *Casual Insomniac* (winner of the 2011 Boom Chapbook Contest, from Bateau Press) and holds degrees from Wittenberg University and UC-Davis. His poems and essays appear in *Southern Review, Pleiades, DIAGRAM, Beloit Poetry Journal, Southeast Review, Hayden's Ferry Review,* and others. He is currently completing a PhD in Literature and Creative Writing at the University of Houston, where he has served as Non-Fiction Editor of *Gulf Coast,* on the faculty for the BoldFACE Writer's Conference and Writers in the Schools.

www.ingramcontent.com/pod-product-compliance
Lightning Source LLC
Chambersburg PA
CBHW022348040426
42449CB00006B/778